PREPARED
TO DIE BUT
TOTALLY
UNPREPARED
TO
LIVE

PREPARED
TO DIE BUT
TOTALLY
UNPREPARED
TO
LIVE

JOHN PHILIP LIBERTO

XULON PRESS

Xulon Press
2301 Lucien Way #415
Maitland, FL 32751
407.339.4217
www.xulonpress.com

Unless otherwise indicated, Scripture quotations taken from the Holy Bible, New International Version (NIV). Copyright © 1973, 1978, 1984, 2011 by Biblica, Inc.™. Used by permission. All rights reserved.

Printed in the United States of America.

ISBN-13: 978-1-54566-290-8

DEDICATION

I dedicate this book to my grandchildren;
Carter and Ellen Liberto and Jenson
and Jennings Butler.

ACKNOWLEDGEMENTS

I COULD NOT HAVE WRITTEN MY STORY without the inspiration from my wife Sandra who lived the journey with me. Also I want to thank Betty Disher for the many hours she spent editing my story and correcting my sentence structures and punctuation.

INTRODUCTION

WHILE SITTING ON MY BACKYARD DECK early one morning, my eyes kept being drawn to the tire swing that my wife, Sandra, and I had built for our grandkids; I was reminded of how building that tire swing had saved my life. It all began on Friday, March 9th of 2018. Our entire family was in town that weekend to celebrate my granddaughter Ellen's second birthday. I was rushing to get the swing finished. The heavy timber frame had been completed and was anchored in concrete. The only thing left to do was to attach the tire to the chains, but every time I tried to lift the tire I got a severe pain in my back and right side. I thought that I might have pulled a muscle or developed a hernia, but the pain got so intense that I couldn't walk or even move. Sandra called my doctor, and she was told to call 911.

After I arrived at the ER at WakeMed Hospital in Cary, NC, the doctors immediately began ordering tests and ultrasounds. My daughter, Lauren, who was very pregnant at the time, was with me while Sandra was with the grandkids somewhere else. I remember the nurse seemed very concerned. Within an hour of our arrival she told us that my wife needed to come to the hospital immediately. So Sandra got our son-in-law, Jason, to watch the kids, and she and my son, Jeff, soon arrived. Within minutes the ER doctor came in and put his hand on my left shoulder as I lay on the bed. He then calmly said, " I have very bad news. You have cancer. It's a very rare form, and it's very large.

He said that it was called a Liposarcoma and that only a few doctors in the area were experts of that type of cancer. Only Duke University Hospital and The University of No. Carolina Hospital had the doctors that could help me. He said someone would get in touch with us soon. After a few more words of comfort we were sent home in shock with a powerful pain medication. It took a couple days for the the shock to wear off and for someone to contact us. My journey had begun. But if I hadn't hurt myself lifting that tire, the hidden killer would not have been found. And I'm now thankful for that pain.

(Several months latter it was determined by the Veterans Administration that my contact with Agent Orange during the Vietnam War was probably the root cause of my cancer and that it had been growing undetected for many years.)

WINNING THE LOTTERY

IT WAS LIKE WINNING THE LOTTERY BUT only in reverse. The odds were very high and we found out that only two men in a million have the type of Liposarcoma that I had. Only one in a thousand people are born with only one kidney as I was. I can't do the math forward but the odds are astronomical that a person born with only one kidney would have that one kidney completely surrounded by a very rare cancer in such a way that the kidney would have to be completely removed. But I was that person. My number had been called leaving me totally dependent on others to keep me alive through dialysis three times a week for the rest of my life. Talk about bad luck. Talk about getting a raw deal. Talk about coincidences or was it ?

That morning while sitting on my backyard deck these Bible verses kept running through my mind : "...before I formed you in the womb I knew you..." (Jer. 1:5), "...we know that all things work together for good to those who love God according to His purpose. " (Rom 8:28), and

"....not a sparrow will fall to the ground without our Father's knowledge,...you are worth more than many sparrows. "(Matt 10:29-31 paraphrased). So now I'm beginning to wonder if, back in 1946 when I was born, God was already preparing me for my 2018 journey, and it was no coincidence at all but all planned for his own purpose.

UNC CANCER HOSPITAL

WE WERE WAITING FOR A CALL EITHER from Duke or UNC, and it turned out to be UNC. The chief of surgery at UNC Cancer Hospital wanted to meet with us and within two weeks we were in his office in Chapel Hill, NC. We were very familiar with the Hospital complex there because five years earlier we had traveled several times from our current home in Florida to Chapel Hill to see our premature twin grandkids, Carter and Stella. They would be in the NIC Unit there for three months. It brought back both good and bad memories of holding little Stella with all of her life support tubes. She was about the size of a squirrel, and I remember looking down at that beautiful tiny face for the last time.

Dr. Kim told us that he was the expert in the area for the rare cancer that I had, and he wanted to handle it himself instead of assigning another surgeon to me. Jeff and Sandra were there that first meeting when the surgeon told us that the cancer was in the fatty area surrounding all the organs on my right side, except the lung and that it took up approximately 3/4 of my chest cavity. He said its size was not a record but it was one of the largest he had ever seen and estimated it to weigh between ten and twelve pounds. He was very confident and repeatedly told us, "I'm your man. I got this, but I can't save your kidney." That meant I'd be on dialysis the rest of my life. I asked him what other options I had. He calmly answered, " You can die a slow painful death. " That meant I really had no other options. He said he would meet with his surgery team and get back with us in a few days with a plan of attack.

PLAN OF ATTACK

AFTER SEVERAL CONSULTATIONS WITH other doctors we signed stacks of legal documents. Each consultation looked more like a closing for buying a new house than a plan of attack on my cancer, but after two full months since being diagnosed we finally had a plan. Beginning on May 3rd, just three days after my new grandson was born, and continuing for the next five weeks, I would receive daily radiation treatments at the UNC Cancer Hospital in Chapel Hill. That would be followed by seven weeks of just allowing the radiation to cool down and complete its work. The intent was to kill cancer cells and to crystallize the edges of the mass so it could be scraped more easily from the surrounded organs and blood vessels.

Later would come the estimated 10-hour surgery to remove all the cancer and my incapsulated kidney. We were told that it would be a teaching surgery, and we agreed and signed off to allow students and interns in the operating room. One day before radiation was to begin, I was strapped to a bed under the computerized radiation machine. The machine projected an outline of my cancer onto my chest and right side. The technicians then used a permanent green marker to outline its shape on my skin. Sandra correctly said that its shape looked like a large tattoo of Arkansas with four surveying marks as bullseyes to line up the machine before each treatment. One each was to the left and right sides and top of my chest and lower abdomen.

After just a few radiation treatments, as expected, I began experiencing extreme fatigue and weakness and could no longer drive myself back and forth to Chapel Hill. Then Sandra mostly began to drive me, but Jeff and family friends also offered to help. On the morning of June 7th, Jeff joined Sandra and me in Chapel Hill. It was my last day of radiation treatment and I was actually surprised at how fast the five weeks had passed. I was about to turn in my treatment card and bash the brass gong in the waiting room with a wooden mallet as hard as I could signaling I had completed my treatments. Jeff took pictures and a video as I woke up everyone around that area of the hospital with that gong.

PRE-SURGERY CONSULTATIONS

AS WE WAITED FOR THE SURGERY DATE, the next seven weeks also passed quickly. We made day trips and spent time with family and friends. We also traveled to Memphis for my mother's funeral even though I had begun to experience sharp pain and a burning sensation in my abdomen and right side. There were also more consultations and every doctor on the team that we met with explained the risks involved with his or her part of the surgery. They all had us sign off on each one of the risks. We now knew everything that could possibly go wrong during and after surgery.

Most of the doctors said the odds were in my favor, but I remember they ALL said I should, " Expect the best but be prepared for the worst. " One of them even said, " One little slip, and I could fill your chest cavity with blood, " and that statement stuck with me . So many things could possibly go wrong. As an architect, I had practiced designing for the worst possible scenario. The intent was to design exits and travel distances according to building codes so that the most distant person in a building could escape a fire. I began preparing for the worst, and I became convinced that I would not survive the surgery.

We were also told that the cancer had actually grown during the cooling off period. Even as my family and friends were praying for a successful surgery, I began preparing them for the worst. Lauren and Jeff were given copies of all of our legal and financial records. I instructed Sandra how and when to pay the bills because I had always paid them in the past. She learned my method of how to sort out paid and unpaid bills, where the files and envelops were in my desk, etc. And the very next day she taught me her method and how SHE was going to pay everything from then on—online.

I told her whom to hire to take care of the yard because it was too big for her alone. I even discussed with her that she should sell one of the cars. She wouldn't need two without me. Maybe she should sell both and get a newer, bigger one that would accommodate more child seats. Maybe she should even sell the house and buy a smaller one. I went over everything. I can now remember that I took the thought that I was going to die during surgery to the extreme.

DEVOTIONALS

MY DAILY DEVOTIONALS BEGAN TO TAKE on more meaning. I had been saved and baptized as an eleven year old boy. I was raised in a Christian home and always went to church. I had mostly Christian friends, but I must confess that during my early adult life there were several years when I could have been called a hypocrite or a mediocre Christian or something else. But I always knew God was there for me. I was thankful that I had not died suddenly but had plenty of time to look back on my life and get things right.

I knew more than ever that Jesus had died for me so that I could have eternal life. The devotions became deeper and I felt at times that God was in the same room with me. I had deep assurance that all was well with my soul. I remember one morning I thanked God for the peace I had and reminded Him that I had done everything I could do to prepare to die. Later I went to brush my teeth. I was looking in the mirror and listening to the sound of my electric toothbrush.

It came out of nowhere and hit me like a punch on the side of my head. I didn't see any bright lights or hear any voices but God told me clearly, " You've done nothing. I've done it all. " And I felt like the Joker after Batman had punched him for saying something stupid...ZAP !..POW !...WHAM !..., but I got over it. Next I began to prepare God for my pending death. I told him all my concerns for Sandra, Lauren and Jeff, and their spouses. I named all of the grandkids and wondered how they would ever make it without my being there for them.

Just then it suddenly happened again. It was like a another holy punch out of nowhere...KABOOM !...POP !..ZAP !..., and He told me, " I've got this. Do you really think you can guide and protect them better than I can ? " The peace continued to get deeper. I was convinced more than ever that His plan was that I would die during surgery and that God would take care of my family. I remember that I then went to take a nap.

PREPARING
FOR THE WORST

SANDRA AND I BEGAN TO SHOP FOR A cemetery lot the week before the scheduled surgery. We visited several cemeteries in the area and settled on a beautiful one in Apex about 15 miles from our house. It had a veterans' section with a tall flag pole and a couple sculptures. There was also a small chapel. So we bought the lot and designed the brass memorial head marker with simply my name and Army Vietnam Veteran, 1946-2018. The next day we chose where the service would be in a chapel about three miles away.

All this time I was totally convinced that I would die during surgery despite all the prayers going up for me. At the same time I had that very deep peace and assurance that all was well with my soul. We pre-paid for my service. It would be a military service with three active duty soldiers in attendance. Taps would be played at the grave site. We decided to get two folded flags, one to be presented to Lauren and one to Jeff. I picked out a soloist I wanted to sing, and the song I wanted sung, " Come Thou Fount of Every Blessing. " I picked out a minister to perform the service and, we went over the details.

I told her I wasn't sure if we should have the young grand-kids there or not. She looked directly into my eyes and said, " Why not, John ? They will probably all be in high school by then. " I knew that I had found the right minister. Next, Sandra and I discussed who would be the pall bearers. She decided that they would wear coats instead of causal dress. We checked out hotels since virtually all of our relatives live in other states. We decided that hotels in Apex would be better than Fuquay-Varina. We covered everything, everything, and then I was ready to go to Skipper's and eat catfish.

SURGERY

SANDRA AND I STAYED AT THE ALOFT Hotel in Chapel Hill on Wednesday night near the hospital so that we wouldn't be late for surgery the next morning, July 26th. We arrived at 6:00 AM for the 8:00 surgery, the first scheduled for the day. Lauren and Jeff were there with Sandra when Dr. Kim came to see me. I understand that a few friends arrived later and remained during the surgery. It took about two hours to get all my vitals and a gown big enough to cover my backside, and then it was time to go. We all shed tears and hugs. I was thinking that the next time I saw them would be in Heaven, but they were all confident since literally hundreds of people were praying for me, that all would go well.

I never saw so many lights. I remember that the operating room had several very serious-looking nurses busily preparing the instruments. I also remember that the operating table was very narrow, and two attendants made sure I didn't fall off one way or the other as they tried to position me in the center. I remember looking around trying to see if I could identify the physicist who we were told would be in the room to program the radiation machine during surgery to blast areas that wouldn't come loose. But the only person I could identify was the anesthesiologist. I never saw Dr. Kim in surgery. I know I've said this too many times already but I had a very deep peace and knew beyond any doubt that all was well with my soul. There was no fear at all.

I expected to wake up in Heaven, and I had made a mental list of the first few things I wanted to do when I arrived in Heaven. First, I wanted to thank Jesus for all the pain and agony that he suffered for me and for not giving up on me. Second, I wanted to meet the family members that had preceded me. Third, I wanted to tour our Father's mansion to see if it complied with the Americans With Disabilities Act. (I'm just kidding). And fourth, to see Stella. I wondered if she was still a baby or a child or if she had matured. Either way I wanted her to sit on my lap and to call me Papa and then tell me all that she had been up to the past five years. Then it was lights out for me.

THAT BRIGHT LIGHT

LATER I FOUND OUT THAT THE SURGERY went well with very little or no complications. Instead of the estimated ten hours, it was completed in about six and a half hours. Doctors found that the liposarcoma wasn't wrapped as tightly around the vena cava as expected. Dr. Kim was able to get all the cancer out in a blob weighing exactly fifteen pounds. That blob also included my only kidney, my gall bladder, part of my diaphragm, and part of my adrenal gland. Dr. Kim later sent us a picture of the huge red blob which I've shared with only a few people. He said that he would use it for research.

Many people who encounter a near death experience say that they saw a bright light, and I can honestly say that I saw that bright light. I'm not sure if I was unconscious or semi-conscious or what. It was blurry, but was bright and it was directly over my head. There were a couple of angels on the right side of me dressed in blue smocks, and they seemed to be very busy. They never spoke. On my left was a host of more angels, maybe five or six dressed in white coats. The tallest angel on the left did all the talking and prodding. One of the angels in white took notes while the rest stood still with their hands clasped together in front of them. As they began to leave, I thought I saw that they all had stethoscopes and ID badges. And then the bright light went off.

As I lay there, my head was in a fog. I slowly began to realize that I wasn't in Heaven but somewhere else. How could that possibly be ? I could hear people talking but couldn't tell who they were. I was dazed, confused. Something had gone wrong; very wrong. Sandra was leaning over me saying over and over again, " Wake up it's all over; Wake up it's all over. " There were Jeff and Jenna, Lauren and Jason, Carl and Ann, Wayne and Terry, all staring at me. They were all so happy and I finally realized that the surgery was over and I was still alive. I was sorry and happy and scared all at the same time. Now looking back I realize that I was prepared to die, but totally unprepared to live.

QUESTIONING GOD

HOW MANY TIMES DID WE HEAR RICKY
Ricardo of the old I Love Lucy Show tell his wife, " Lucy,
you got some 'splaining to do ? " Well over the next few
weeks, I began to foolishly think that God had some
'splaining to do to me. I thought we had an agreement.
I felt betrayed, and I was angry at God. How could He
have done this to me ? He knew that I didn't want the
after-surgery life that I was destined to have if I survived
the surgery with no kidneys. I would be totally dependent
on others to keep me alive while attached to a dialysis
machine three times a week. I had loss my physical independence and dignity.

Apparently God and I weren't on the same page. I thought
the deal was that I would die during surgery and escape
all the pain and discomfort post surgery. I would immediately enter Heaven and He would take care of my family.
There was that deep peace and assurance which I inter-
preted as His stamp of approval. But I was still alive.
How could I ever trust Him again ? At the same time I

was thanking Him for answering the prayers of all those praying for me. It truly was a miracle. I was totally confused. All I wanted to do was to take my pain meds and sleep to escape reality.

All the grandkids came to see me in the hospital. I was so glad to see them because they made me happy. At the same time I really didn't want them to see me like that. I ended up spending fifteen days in the hospital in Chapel Hill, one of the best hospitals in the country with the best doctors and nurses available. I was fortunate to be there but I was miserable. I was in pain and swollen in places that I didn't know could get swollen. Sandra was with me day and night. Lauren was there a few days also.

When Jeff wasn't working, he would step in for Sandra at night so she could go to the hotel for a shower and a good night's sleep. Both Jeff and Sandra said that I struggled in my sleep by constantly moaning and talking to someone. I can remember some nightmares apparently caused by the pain meds. Meanwhile I had my first few dialysis sessions while in the hospital, and all of them were miserable experiences. I was getting more and more bitter and agitated. I remember again that I foolishly thought it was all God's fault and that He had some ' splaining to do to me.

REHAB

AFTER I WAS DISCHARGED FROM THE hospital, I was transported to a rehab facility where I continued feeling extremely sorry for myself. One night I was lying alone in my room. I was just thinking; no tv or music playing. I was just alone in the dark when I remembered something that happened a couple months before. Sandra and I had gone to Ruby Tuesday's after church for lunch, and as we were leaving we passed Toys R Us which was having a going-out-of-business sale. Sandra decided to go inside and look for some bargains for the grandkids. I stayed in the car which was parked in the first handicap spot from the door where I could see everyone going in or out.

Soon, I noticed a young mom walking in front of her seven or eight year-old son. They were headed for the store. He was wearing dark glasses and was using a child's version of a blind man's walking stick. His mother was constantly talking to him, but there was no physical contact between them. He was on his own tapping his cane left to right in front of himself and then turning at just the right time to enter the store behind his mother. I admired how she was teaching him to be independent at a very early age, but I felt sorry for the boy and said a little prayer for him. I also thanked God that I had nearly seventy-two years of good eyesight to see all the beauty of His creations and that if I suddenly lost my sight I would have nothing to complain about.

Within a couple minutes of their entering the store, a van pulled into the handicap space across the aisle from me. Soon, a young couple and their two young daughters exited the van. The father then pulled a ramp down from the side door and wheeled a child's wheelchair down to the pavement. The four or five year old boy in the chair obviously had extreme physical problems. He was slowly swinging his arms and head around. Each of the girls held onto one side of the chair as the father slowly wheeled him into the store. Again, I felt sorry for this child and said a quick prayer for him. I then thanked God that I didn't have problems like that. But if after over seventy one years of good health I suddenly was wheelchair-bound, I would have nothing to complain about.

I'm thinking you probably know where I'm heading with this. Yep, just a couple months later, after nearly seventy two years of good health, my life WAS suddenly turned upside down and changed forever. As I sat alone in the dark that night in my room I realized that when I faced the reality of losing my physical freedom, I did begin to complain. I complained a lot even after I had been blessed with so many years of good health. Now I realize that I'm a hypocrite and that I'm sorrier for my own situation than I was for those kids.

NURSING HOME

THEY CALLED IT A REHAB FACILITY. Technically, it probably was, but to me it was a nursing home. Both my father and mother had lived in one during their later years until they died. I was told that I could be there up to six weeks, six long miserable weeks in a nursing home ! Sandra kept telling me, "You don't need six weeks. We're getting you out of here in three weeks." That motivated me and made me work harder to get out more quickly.

By far I was the youngest of the approximately two hundred residents that I saw there. I was probably ten to twenty years younger then most of them. I could see through open doors that some lay on their beds staring at the ceiling. Dozens of others sat in their wheelchairs in the corridors, and many gathered at the nurses' stations for no apparent reason other than they had no other place to go. None of them were talking to each other but just sitting there with blank looks on their faces.

Most of them appeared too weak to move their wheel-chairs with their arms but they were able to do an extremely slow shuffle with their feet to propel themselves a couple feet at a time. Then they would drop their heads to stare at the floor or take a nap—something I had seen my mother do many times before. It reminded me of my sister's devotion to checking on my mother daily for years. Now that's where I found myself with Sandra's spending most of every day caring for me.

THERAPY

I HAD HOURS OF PHYSICAL AND OCCUPA-tional therapy daily. Soon I had learned how to get in and out of my wheelchair and bed by myself, how to go to the bathroom, how to take a shower sitting down, how to shave, and how to dress myself. Soon I was being wheeled down the maze of corridors to the therapy room in the next wing. That's where the therapy got more intense. I remember I was more determined than ever to get out of there.

Meanwhile on Mondays, Wednesdays, and Fridays, a rehab driver would take me from my room in my wheel-chair and deliver me to the dialysis center three miles away via a handicap van. There after ten minutes of preparation, I would lie still for the next four hours as the dialysis machine did its thing. Then it took ten more minutes to be disconnected before being transported back to my room. I felt so helpless and totally dependent on others.

In the therapy room for two hours a day, I was making progress. I could ride the stationary bike for thirty minutes. I began to stand holding onto a rail. Soon I was stacking plastic cups while standing and grabbing the rail just before losing my balance. In their kitchen I learned to get cups and food out of cabinets and fix myself a sandwich. I was taught how to get myself into and out of a car, how to climb steps, and how to find marbles in play dough. (Don't ask me why).

FRUSTRATIONS

ALL THE DOCTORS AND NURSES AND even the therapist kept telling me that I was in excellent shape and that I had the body of a sixty year-old instead of a seventy-one year old. That made me feel hopeful for recovery but my mind and attitude were in the tank. I had given God the silent treatment for a long time but I began to take my frustrations out on the one who helped me the most. She was the one who was with me every day and night in the hospital.

She was the one who wiped my brow with a cool cloth when I was sweating with pain, the one who played Bill Gaither music to soothe me to sleep, the one who held my hand and prayed for me over and over again with tears streaming down her face, the one who read Bible passages to comfort me and read every one of the dozens of cards I received from family and friends and even strangers; the one who was constantly assuring me that my situation was only temporary and things would soon get better. But I began to complain to her about everything.

I didn't like the way she fixed my window blinds. I didn't like the way she arranged my stuff on my bedside table. I didn't like the clothes she brought me, etc, etc. After a few days she finally couldn't take it anymore and told me she was leaving, and she did. She left me alone, and I really couldn't blame her. I hated the man that I had become and that irritated me even more. Early the next morning there was a knock on my door, and in walked Sandra. She was back. As the politicians or professional athletes or movie stars caught for some misdeed, I now remember saying to myself, "That's not the man I am. That's not the real me."

GOING HOME

ABOUT THAT TIME, I BEGAN TO SEE A LIGHT
at the end of the tunnel. I was dismissed from the rehab
center after only three weeks. Sandra's prediction had
come true. She packed up all my belongings and drove
me home, and it was a great feeling. Friends had hung
yellow ribbons to welcome me home. I was primally using
my Rollator by then and had a little trouble getting up the
ramp in the garage but I was finally at home and sleeping
in my own bed again.

The home therapy continued for three more weeks with
two different therapists for a total of four hours a week.
Sandra continued taking me to dialysis on Mondays,
Wednesdays, and Fridays. Friends, family, and neigh-
bors began to stop by to see me, but, best of all the grandkids began coming by to see me again. They all wanted
to see my boo boo and asked if I was getting better. I
still felt tired most of the time, but I was beginning to be
happy to be alive again and was finally getting out of that
dark place.

I began my devotionals again to see if I could re-connect with God. I was ready to move on and within seconds of that very first devotional it was as if He was right there with me again. He was just waiting for me to come back. I told God that I meant no disrespect to Him with my critical ' sitting on my deck in the Quay ' post that I had put out on Facebook, But that I was just trying to record my true feelings. Over time the frustrations began to leave, and that deep peace eventually returned. Then I began to pray about the big white elephant in the room, dialysis. I hated those long four-hour sessions, and something had to be done.

Sandra came up with a brilliant idea. She said that many retirees get bored and take on a part time job just to stay busy. She suggested that my dialysis sessions could be likened to a post retirement job. It would be just three days a week and a total of just twelve hours. I thought that was a great idea and I decided to try it. I even began to dress up a little bit whenever I went to my new job with slacks and a button down collar shirt. It wasn't a blue vest with the yellow Walmart logo on the back. I wasn't greeting customers going in and out of a store, but I began to like my new job.

DIALYSIS

MY DIALYSIS CENTER HAS A MORNING and an afternoon shift. There are about thirty of us patients in each shift with about seven or eight technicians who operate the computerized machines we are each connected to. Most technicians are dressed in plastic protective gowns with plastic face shields. Alarms are constantly sounding, and the technicians are moving from one patient to another pushing buttons and resetting things. There are also three nurses and a physician's assistant in the room for emergencies.

Time was my worst enemy while I was lying still for four straight hours. But I soon learned to manage the time. I began to spend one hour reading, one listening to podcasts, one napping and the last hour watching tv. The time began flying by and now some days I can't wait to get to my new " job." It's no longer a dreaded experience. Also I've gotten most of my independence back. I'm now physically well enough to drive myself back and forth to dialysis. I've even stopped by the grocery store on my way home to pick up a few items and a dozen daises for Sandra the other day.

I've never been the most outgoing or friendliest person, but I began to strike up conversations with each of the personnel taking care of me. I even began getting to know the nurses and the PA. Soon we were sharing pictures and stories about our families. Most of the patients don't talk to each other during sessions even though they are only four feet apart. They usually have ear plugs on and are watching tv or sleeping, but I've been able to strike up a conversation with a couple of them in the lobby.

SPIRITUAL
LESSONS LEARNED

A FEW DAYS AFTER THANKSGIVING, WHILE putting up garland and Christmas lights on our fence, I was listening to music on my iPhone. The 1970s hit " Like a Bridge Over Troubled Water " by Simon and Garfunkel was playing. I began thinking about all the troubled water in my life this past year, but I don't remember ever looking down at it from the safety of a bridge. I was always in the middle of it. That reminded me that God never promised to give us a trouble free life but he would be there for us in times of trouble. Looking back I can truly say he was with me all the way even though I didn't always realize it at the time.

I'm not sure what direction all of this is leading me, but I am sure my story will continue in some way. God didn't extend my life without a purpose. He has let me know that He wants me to be light and salt wherever I go. For now I seem to be in a holding pattern, and I'm waiting for guidance. I'm definitely over the hump and I'm quickly adjusting to my new norms. I realize I'm beginning to look forward more than I'm looking backward, and I'm now trying to be just as prepared to live as I was to die a few months ago. I know God has preformed a great miracle in my life and I want to thank Him in a great and unique way. Not with a cliche. For now all I can come up with is....." God is faithful. "

PREPARED TO DIE BUT TOTALLY
UNPREPARED TO LIVE